# Maine Coast Collection

Forts of Maine

Lighthouses of Maine

Maine Seabirds: Past and Present

Maine's Rocky Coast

Sea Glass

**Homeschoolers of Maine**
P.O. Box 159, Camden, ME 04843
Telephone: 207.763.2880   Email: homeschl@midcoast.com
www.homeschoolersofmaine.org

# Table of Contents

Each unit study contains its own individual table of content.  In that you will find specifics for that individual study.

# INTRODUCTION

Homeschoolers of Maine (HOME) is a statewide 501(c)3 non-profit, ministry-based organization, and was founded on the belief that all families have a God-given and constitutional right and responsibility to direct the education of their children, regardless of their educational philosophy or religious affiliation.

Our mission is to:

**Preserve** parent-led home education
**Protect** homeschool freedoms, and
**Promote** safe and healthy learning environments.

Thank you for supporting Homeschoolers of Maine by choosing one of our carefully constructed unit studies for your student.

In each unit study, HOME strives to provide at least one question or activity within each of the required subject areas: Math, Language Arts, Social Studies, Science, Health, Physical Education, Maine Studies, Computer, Library Skills, and Fine Arts. Bible is also included, and occasionally Foreign Language, for those who would like to cover those additional areas. This helps to illustrate how a study on a single subject can cover multiple required areas.

This bundle is not a conclusive study of the subject but is intended to spark the student's interest by asking them questions and providing them with basic direction in which to begin pursuing their study of the subject. In most cases, it does not contain answers to the questions asked. This is intentional. Our unit studies are designed to help students explore, discover and develop their own perspective on various subjects that are of interest to them.

Students should in no way be confined to the questions and activities contained here. If their level of interest widens or veers off in another direction, encourage them to follow their passion.

# OVERVIEW

## Lighthouses of Maine

Maine has 70 lighthouses! Each one has its own unique story. If you're looking for something fun and educational to do this summer, consider taking a trip along the coast of Maine and learning about some of these lighthouses up close and in person. This unit study takes a general look at the things you can learn at stops along the way.

You will want a copy of the current *The Original Discovering Maine's Lighthouses and Harbors* published each summer by Courier Publications, LLC, and available free in many local stores and libraries. This will be your guide to the lighthouses of Maine.

## Maine Forts

This unit study is a generic format that allows students to explore one, several or all of the forts that once were (and in some cases still remain) along Maine's coastline.

Maine's coastline is rich with historic fort locations. Many of the forts no longer exist, but the sites remain.

This unit study is designed to be done on a specific fort. It can be done, though, for each fort that the student is interested in learning about.

http://www.travel-maine.info/historic_forts.htm, http://www.fortwiki.com/Category:Maine_All
http://www.northamericanforts.com/East/me.html

The above websites contain lists of all the forts in Maine. Any one of these is a good starting point.

## Maine's Rocky Coast

This unit study will take you on an adventure exploring Maine's rocky coastline as you study geography, natural science, marine life, and so much more. You'll find lots of great field trip ideas and educational opportunities to take along to the beach with you this summer!

## Maine Sea Birds: Past and Present

Working through this study, you will explore the enchanting seabirds of Maine, including the now extinct Great Auk. This is a great opportunity to talk about conservation and preservation of currently existing species that may be threatened. If you include field trips, it will take students out onto the rocky shore allowing them firsthand opportunities to watch the amazing creatures that inhabit the Maine coastline.

You may want to consider downloading and printing this free 26 page guide to Maine Seabirds to use during the course of this study.
https://www.fws.gov/uploadedFiles/Region_5/NWRS/North_Zone/Maine_Coastal_Islands/Guide%20to%20Maine%20Seabirds_opt.pdf

## Sea Glass

In this study, students will explore natural and man-made sea glass. There is an abundance of resources on the subject, and it's both beautiful and fun. Who knew a trip to the beach could cover so much schooling?

# Lighthouses of Maine

## Table of Contents:

## Before You Begin

Sometimes it can be challenging to figure out how to show progress when a student is working on a unit study. Before you begin this study, ask the student to give you a brief narrative of what they already know about the subject of this HOME unit study. Write this out for younger students, have older students write it out for themselves, here. When you finish the study, there is a page at the end entitled, **What I Learned,** for students to write down new things that they learned during the study. The comparison of these two pages can be used for portfolio reviews to document that progress in learning was made by the student.

_____
_____
_____
_____
_____
_____
_____
_____
_____
_____
_____
_____
_____
_____
_____
_____
_____
_____
_____
_____
_____
_____
_____
_____
_____

Date Begun: _____

www.homeschoolersofmaine.org

# BIBLE

Look up Matthew 5:16. Write it out and memorize it.

_____

_____

_____

_____

What does it mean to "let your light shine?" _____

_____

_____

Give three examples of how you can "shine your light" this week.

1. _____

2. _____

3. _____

Look up John 8:12. Write it out and memorize it.

_____

_____

_____

_____

_____

How is a lighthouse like Jesus?

_____

_____

_____

_____

_____

# MATH

Using the graph on the next page, choose ten lighthouses that you have visited or would like to visit and list the height of each. Record the height of each on the graph.

1. _____     6. _____

2. _____     7. _____

3. _____     8. _____

4. _____     9. _____

5. _____     10. _____


What is the average height of the lighthouses you chose? _____

Which lighthouse is the tallest? _____

How tall is the tallest lighthouse? _____

Which lighthouse is the shortest? _____

How tall is the shortest lighthouse? _____

How much taller is the tallest lighthouse than the shortest? _____

Which lighthouse would you most like to visit? _____

How far is it from your house? _____

If you travel 50 miles per hour, how long will it take you to get there? _____

**Height**

200 ft.

180 ft.

160 ft

140 ft.

120 ft

100 ft.

80 ft.

60 ft

40 ft.

20 ft.

**Name of Lighthouse**

# LANGUAGE ARTS

Unscramble the following vocabulary words.

**lesfner slne** _____
_____
_____

**scato dugra** _____
_____
_____

**elsiguhoht** _____
_____
_____

**dinlas** _____
_____
_____

**kraeb teawr** _____
_____
_____

**deha thlig** _____
_____
_____

**beecaarono** _____
_____
_____

**tinaucla** _____
_____
_____

**tiiramem**_____
_____
_____

Answers are at the end of the unit study.

Once you've unscrambled each work, look up and write out a definition for the term.

There are 70 lighthouses in Maine. Choose one to learn more about. When was it built? Who were the lighthouse keepers? Is it still used today? Include any other facts or details you find interesting.

_____
_____
_____
_____
_____
_____
_____
_____
_____
_____
_____
_____
_____
_____
_____
_____
_____
_____
_____
_____
_____

Read Keep the Lights Burning, Abbie by Connie Rood. Write a journal entry that depicts one day in the life of a light-house keeper, or what you imagine it might be.

_____
_____
_____
_____
_____
_____
_____
_____
_____
_____
_____

# SOCIAL STUDIES

Look up and learn about the following individuals.  Choose one to write a brief biography on.

Augustine Fresnel

Marcus Hanna

Abbie Burgess

_____
_____
_____
_____
_____
_____
_____
_____
_____
_____

Visit the following website and learn about women who worked as lighthouse keepers.  How many of the women listed were from Maine?
https://www.history.uscg.mil/Browse-by-Topic/Notable-People/Women/Women-Lighthouse-Keepers/

_____
_____
_____
_____
_____
_____

What were the duties of a lighthouse keeper?

_____
_____
_____
_____
_____
_____
_____
_____

There are 70 lighthouses in Maine.  On a map of Maine, locate each of the lighthouses.

## SCIENCE

Look up and learn about the Fresnel Lens. Who invented it? How does it work? Is it still used in modern lighthouses?

_____
_____
_____
_____
_____

Learn about the tides. How often do they change? Did the tides have any impact on the lighthouse or the life of the lighthouse keeper?

_____
_____
_____
_____
_____
_____
_____

Consider what marine life might be found on the shore around the lighthouse. Did the lighthouse keepers take advantage of any of these as food? If so what? Were the species the same in the 1700's and 1800's as they are today? What is missing? What is here now that wasn't then?

_____
_____
_____
_____
_____
_____
_____
_____
_____

# HEALTH/PHYSICAL EDUCATION

What did lighthouse keepers eat?  Where did their food come from?  What did they do if a storm prevented them from accessing the main land?

_____
_____
_____
_____
_____
_____
_____
_____
_____

Visit one or more of Maine's lighthouses. Choose ones that you have to hike to. Plan a day walking on the beach near one of the lighthouses.

Imagine what it must have been like to live in a lighthouse. What types of activities do you think lighthouse keepers might have engaged in?

_____
_____
_____
_____
_____
_____
_____
_____

# COMPUTER/LIBRARY SKILLS

You will use the internet and/or your local library for a great deal of the research for this unit study.

List the various resources you used during the course of your study.

Source Title                                                          Type of Media

_____

_____

_____

_____

_____

_____

_____

_____

_____

_____

_____

_____

_____

_____

_____

_____

_____

_____

_____

_____

_____

_____

_____

_____

_____

_____

_____

**FINE ARTS**

Photograph or paint a lighthouse scene.

Write a poem about a lighthouse.

_____

_____

_____

_____

_____

_____

Look for Maine lighthouses portrayed by Maine artists.  What did you find?  Did you like it?  Why or why not?

_____

_____

_____

_____

_____

_____

_____

_____

_____

Read *Light on Jib Island* by Maine author Jan Gilley and do a book report.

# Book Report

Title: _____

Author: _____

Illustrator: _____

Publisher: _____


Main character(s) in the story: _____

_____

_____


Where does the story take place: _____

_____

_____


What happens during the story: _____

_____

_____

_____

_____

_____

_____


Would you recommend this story to a friend?  Why or why not? _____

_____

_____

_____

_____

# FIELD TRIPS

Watch for Maine Open Lighthouse Day, typically in September. Plan to take advantage of the opportunity to visit a lighthouse near you. Which one did you visit? Write about your visit below.

_____
_____
_____
_____
_____
_____
_____

Create a checklist of Maine lighthouse and see how many you can visit in one season. Write a short essay about your visit.

_____
_____
_____
_____
_____
_____
_____

Visit the Maine Lighthouse Museum in Rockland, Maine. Write about what you learned?

_____
_____
_____
_____
_____
_____
_____
_____
_____

NOTES:

## What I Learned

In this section, ask the student to narrate what they learned that they didn't know when they began this study. What new discovery did they make during the study? What did they enjoy most? What do they know now that they didn't know before? These are all good questions to ask, if the student needs prompting.

_____
_____
_____
_____
_____
_____
_____
_____
_____
_____
_____
_____
_____
_____
_____
_____
_____
_____
_____
_____
_____
_____
_____
_____
_____
_____
_____
_____

Date Completed: _____

NOTES:

# ADDITIONAL RESOURCES

## INTERNET RESOURCES

uslhs.org

lighthousefoundation.org

https://en.wikipedia.org/wiki/List_of_lighthouses_in_Maine

## BOOKS

*Lighthouses for Kids: History, Science, and Lore with 21 Activities*, Katherine L. House
*Abbie Against the Storm: The True Story of a Young Heroine and a Lighthouse,* Marcia K. Vaughan
*A Light in the Storm: The Civil War Diary of Amelia Martin,* Karen Hess

## ANSWERS TO WORD SCRAMBLE

lesfner slne _____ fresnel lens_____

scato dugra _____ coast guard_____

elsiguhoht _____ lighthouse_____

dinlas _____ island_____

kraeb teawr _____ break water_____

deha thlig _____ head light _____

beecaarono _____ aerobeacon_____

tinaucla _____ nautical_____

tiiramem_____ maritime_____

# Maine Forts

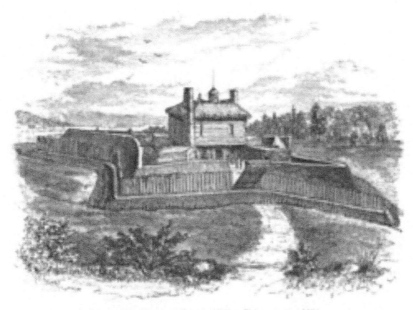

Fort Pownall. Built 1759. Destroyed 1775.

# Table of Contents

## Before You Begin

Sometimes it can be challenging to figure out how to show progress when a student is working on a unit study. Before you begin this study, ask the student to give you a brief narrative of what they already know about the subject of this HOME unit study. Write this out for younger students, have older students write it out for themselves, here. When you finish the study, there is a page at the end entitled, **What I Learned,** for students to write down new things that they learned during the study. The comparison of these two pages can be used for portfolio reviews to document that progress in learning was made by the student.

_____
_____
_____
_____
_____
_____
_____
_____
_____
_____
_____
_____
_____
_____
_____
_____
_____
_____
_____
_____
_____
_____
_____
_____

Date Begun: _____

## BIBLE

Can you find references to forts (fortresses) in the Bible?

_____
_____
_____
_____
_____
_____

In some translations of the Bible, the word stronghold is used.  How many times in the Bible can you find the word stronghold or fort?

_____
_____
_____
_____
_____

What is a fortress or stronghold? _____

_____

Look up, read and memorize  2 Samuel 22:2-3 .

What does this passage say about God? What do you think that means?

_____
_____
_____
_____
_____
_____

# MATH

How far is the fort you have chosen from your home? _____

How long will it take to get there? _____

Figure out the cost of gas for the trip, as well as admission fees and spending money. How much will it cost your family to visit the fort you are studying? Will you need to save for this trip? How much will you need to save each week/month? How long will it take you to save?

_____
_____
_____
_____
_____

What is (or was) the length, width and height of the fort you have chosen to visit? How thick are/were the walls? What shape is/was the fort and was that important to the defense of the fort? If so, why?

_____
_____
_____
_____
_____

Calculate the square footage of the fort based on what you learned about it's length and width.

_____

How many soldiers were garrisoned at the fort? _____

**Vocabulary**

**Define each word and use it in a sentence.**

Garrison _____

_____

_____


Fortify_____

_____

_____


Cavalry _____

_____

_____


Bunker _____

_____

_____


Rampart _____

_____

_____


Siege _____

_____

_____


Blockhouse _____

_____

_____

Write a brief report on the fort you've chosen. Be sure to include information about when it was built, whether or not any wars were fought there, etc.

_____
_____
_____
_____
_____
_____
_____
_____
_____
_____
_____
_____
_____
_____

Research whether any books have been written about the fort you are studying. Are they non-fiction or fiction? How many books are there available? Choose one to read and write a brief book report on.

_____
_____
_____
_____
_____
_____
_____
_____
_____
_____
_____
_____
_____
_____
_____

## SOCIAL STUDIES

What is the geographic location of your fort and why do you think it was built there?

_____
_____
_____
_____
_____

What was the purpose of the fort you are studying?

_____
_____
_____
_____
_____

What was happening in Maine and in the United States during the time when this fort was in use?

_____
_____
_____
_____
_____

Who or what was the fort you've chosen named for?

_____
_____
_____
_____

Were any significant battles fought at this fort? If so, what armies were involved and who won?

_____
_____
_____
_____
_____

# SCIENCE

What type of materials was the fort constructed of?  Is it still standing?

_____

_____

_____

_____

_____

What kind of weaponry was used at this fort?  Who invented the technology?  How was it made?  How did it work?

_____

_____

_____

_____

_____

_____

_____

_____

_____

Research the steps to firing a cannon. Was it the same during the American Revolution as it was during the Civil War?  What was the same? Different?

_____

_____

_____

_____

_____

_____

## HEALTH/PHYSICAL EDUCATION

What illnesses were common during the time the fort was in use? Chose one and describe how it was treated.  Is the illness still around today?  Is it treated differently now than in the past?

_____

_____

_____

_____

_____

_____


Research MRE's (military rations) Does the military still use them today? What was included? What are the benefits of using MREs as a food source for soldiers. _____

_____

_____

_____

_____

_____

_____


Many of the forts in Maine are now part of historic park sites, and have hiking trails.  If the fort you are learning about has trails, plan on taking a hike.  Before hand, consider the length of the trail and what you may want to take along.  Will you need a backpack? Snacks? More than one water bottle? A first-aid kit?

_____

_____

_____

_____

_____

_____

_____

_____

# COMPUTER/LIBRARY SKILLS

You will use the internet and/or your local library for a great deal of the research for this unit study.

List the various resources you used during the course of your study.

Source Title                                                    Type of Media

_____

_____

_____

_____

_____

_____

_____

_____

_____

_____

_____

_____

_____

_____

_____

_____

_____

_____

_____

_____

_____

_____

_____

_____

_____

_____

_____

_____

_____

# FINE ARTS

Look for paintings or old photographs of the fort you've chosen to study. Investigate the artist or photographer. Did they do work representing other Maine forts?

_____
_____
_____
_____
_____

Consider the time period that the fort you've chosen was active. What was the popular music of the time? What instruments might soldiers at the fort have had? Listen to music from that time period that might have been listened to by those at the fort.

_____
_____
_____
_____
_____

Consider drawing or making a scale model of the fort you are studying. Using toy army men, recreate a battle at the model fort.

# MAINE STUDIES

What town is the fort located in? Write a brief history of the town including when it was established, who established it, who the first settlers were, and any other interesting facts you learned.

_____

_____

_____

_____

_____

_____

_____

_____

_____

_____

_____

_____

_____

_____

_____

_____

_____

_____

_____

_____

_____

_____

_____

_____

_____

_____

_____

**FIELD TRIPS**

Visiting any of Maine's historic forts will be a field trip. Include pictures and brochures in your portfolio, from your trip.

# Field Trip Form

Date: _____

Destination: _____

Purpose: _____

Something I saw or learned:

_____
_____
_____
_____
_____
_____
_____
_____
_____

Insert or draw a picture here from your field trip:

# What I Learned

In this section, ask the student to narrate what they learned that they didn't know when they began this study. What new discovery did they make during the study? What did they enjoy most? What do they know now that they didn't know before? These are all good questions to ask, if the student needs prompting.

_____
_____
_____
_____
_____
_____
_____
_____
_____
_____
_____
_____
_____
_____
_____
_____
_____
_____
_____
_____
_____
_____
_____
_____
_____
_____
_____
_____
_____

Date Completed: _____

# Maine's Rocky Coast

# Table of Contents

## Before You Begin

Sometimes it can be challenging to figure out how to show progress when a student is working on a unit study. Before you begin this study, ask the student to give you a brief narrative of what they already know about the subject of this HOME unit study. Write this out for younger students, have older students write it out for themselves, here. When you finish the study, there is a page at the end entitled, **What I Learned,** for students to write down new things that they learned during the study. The comparison of these two pages can be used for portfolio reviews to document that progress in learning was made by the student.

_____
_____
_____
_____
_____
_____
_____
_____
_____
_____
_____
_____
_____
_____
_____
_____
_____
_____
_____
_____
_____
_____
_____
_____

Date Begun: _____

NOTES:

# BIBLE

How many Bible verses can you find about the sea?

_____

_____

_____

_____

_____

Read *The Star Thrower* by Loren Eisley.  You can find it at the link below.

https://www.eiseley.org/Star_Thrower_Cook.pdf

How can we apply the principle to our Christian walk? Explain your answer.

_____

_____

_____

_____

_____

Read *The Legend of the Sea Dollar.* How many Biblical applications are made in this poem?

_____

_____

_____

_____

# MATH

Using a tape measure, mark out a one foot square of the beach you are visiting, count all the periwinkle shells (or other items) in that square foot. Based on the number in that foot, estimate how many there are on the beach all together.

What I chose to count. _____

How many in one small square foot? _____

Estimation of number on the whole beach. _____

Using the same small one foot square, create a graph of all the different types of shells/sea life found in that square.

Name and location of beach I visited. _____

| Item Found/ How many? | | | | | | | | |
|---|---|---|---|---|---|---|---|---|
| | | | | | | | | |
| Twenty-one | | | | | | | | |
| Eighteen | | | | | | | | |
| Fifteen | | | | | | | | |
| Twelve | | | | | | | | |
| Nine | | | | | | | | |
| Six | | | | | | | | |
| Three | | | | | | | | |

What did you find the most of? _____

What did you find the least of? _____

What did you find that was most surprising? _____

What did you hope to find, but didn't? _____

How does a lobsterman determine which lobsters are "keepers"? What are the size requirements and how are they measured?

_____

_____

_____

_____

_____


Approximately how many pounds of lobster are caught annually off the coast of Maine? What percentage of the nation's lobster is caught here in Maine?

_____

_____

_____

_____

_____

## LANGUAGE ARTS

Read *Touch Blue* by Cynthia Lord.  Why is blue sea glass lucky?  Have you ever found a piece of blue sea glass?

_____

_____

_____

_____

_____

Maine author Louise Dickenson Rich wrote *Star Island Boy* in the 1940's.  Read this story.  How is it similar to *Touch Blue*?  How is it different?

_____

_____

_____

_____

_____

_____

_____

_____

Read "The Sandpiper," a poem by Celia Thaxter.  Who is the speaker of the poem?  What is the setting?  Can you find an example of a simile in the poem?  Can you find an example of personification?

_____

_____

_____

_____

_____

_____

_____

# Ocean Word Search

Find the words from the list below in the word search.  If you don't know the meaning of a word, look it up in the dictionary or online.

```
m  s  e  a  l  x  o  x  r  y  m  i  b  d  m  e  i  t  h  k  e  f  b  n  s
x  o  l  e  s  s  u  m  x  n  k  b  d  v  a  l  l  i  o  j  l  a  v  e  h
o  s  o  l  h  i  m  r  m  m  a  s  y  x  l  k  w  e  q  s  r  e  a  t  s
p  l  h  n  j  d  t  n  a  r  o  m  r  o  c  n  a  k  u  c  x  u  h  x  i
g  b  b  w  j  h  f  t  m  l  s  n  p  y  r  i  v  h  t  d  r  s  i  w  f
i  p  a  r  o  e  i  c  y  l  l  v  j  a  x  w  q  i  i  c  e  e  p  i  r
s  h  g  q  s  b  l  t  a  b  p  o  l  a  z  i  m  i  h  d  v  a  e  d  a
q  s  o  o  j  a  m  l  t  g  g  k  d  p  h  r  u  i  j  e  h  g  s  t  t
v  i  o  z  g  q  d  x  y  n  b  p  x  d  e  e  n  t  s  s  q  u  t  q  s
k  b  y  m  s  j  e  c  c  x  p  u  i  h  n  p  o  t  l  l  l  y  o  d
l  f  a  e  h  u  d  e  n  y  h  r  y  h  v  a  j  o  g  l  h  l  u  z  j
j  o  d  g  q  s  r  j  q  u  n  d  o  k  i  l  s  x  y  l  b  k  n  s  q
w  c  b  k  k  b  i  t  u  t  d  r  x  t  v  z  r  d  v  i  o  g  e  u  c
k  e  a  s  n  m  t  r  j  p  s  e  e  u  i  d  a  d  r  s  d  w  m  i  e
g  e  t  n  t  l  p  x  i  e  s  f  l  e  v  k  z  j  h  x  b  w  l  l  l
t  v  l  a  x  e  b  x  s  a  p  y  w  j  g  b  o  i  u  d  n  i  c  x  j
n  y  b  p  y  a  r  h  r  o  c  k  w  e  e  d  r  z  h  d  m  a  l  m  d
w  u  b  z  r  y  o  z  l  c  x  l  g  k  h  p  c  z  r  p  n  b  r  w  a
f  t  i  c  q  e  q  f  f  o  h  d  y  c  q  h  l  b  e  r  f  f  d  a  d
n  f  c  l  c  g  n  w  d  o  s  l  g  t  t  n  a  t  a  k  g  q  f  w  p
p  i  q  r  a  g  z  c  v  n  f  m  p  y  f  y  m  b  a  i  j  v  n  n  x
a  t  a  o  r  q  s  e  a  l  e  t  t  u  c  e  r  w  z  c  j  z  d  d  t
i  b  u  n  c  g  q  m  v  i  q  w  v  l  l  e  h  s  r  e  p  p  i  l  s
d  c  f  s  u  i  h  o  g  f  u  r  p  o  e  v  m  x  a  q  f  n  j  g  m
t  p  b  b  j  c  a  c  o  r  a  d  q  z  k  b  u  f  b  l  y  z  h  g  e
```

| | |
|---|---|
| barnacle | periwinkle |
| clam | razor clam |
| cormorant | rockweed |
| crab | sand dollar |
| hermit crab | seagull |
| horseshoe crab | seal |
| rish moss | sea lettuce |
| Kelp | sea urchin |
| Limpet | slipper shell |
| Lobster | starfish |
| moon jelly | whelk |
| mussel | |

# SOCIAL STUDIES

What is a prevailing wind?

_____

_____

_____

_____

_____


Why is the northern coastal region of Maine called "Down East Maine"?

_____

_____

_____

_____

_____


How does the Maine coastline vary?  What are different geographical features that make up the coast line?

_____

_____

_____

_____

_____

Find and name a location along Maine's coast for each of the following:

Estuary _____

Salt Marsh _____

Tidal Flat _____

Delta _____

Beach _____

Dune _____


Choose one of the words above that you aren't familiar with to research further. Record what you found?

_____
_____
_____
_____
_____
_____
_____
_____
_____

# SCIENCE

Have you seen a lobster that is different colors on each half?  Research why this happens.  How are these lobsters different than lobsters that are all one color?

_____

_____

_____

_____

_____

What happens to crabs, periwinkles, hermit crabs and starfish during the winter?

_____

_____

_____

_____

_____

Learn about the ebb and flow of the tide.  What makes the tide high and low?  Why is it different each day?  Why is it important to know if the tide will be high or low at a certain time?

If you're looking for resources on how the tide works, consider watching various videos available on YouTube.

_____

_____

_____

_____

_____

There were once penguins in Maine. They were called the Great Auk. The Great Auk is now extinct. Research the Great Auk. What did it look like? What was it used for? Why did it become extinct?

_____
_____
_____
_____
_____
_____
_____
_____
_____
_____

What natural resources are being harvested from the Maine ocean today? Is there any chance of any of these things becoming extinct? Why/why not?

_____
_____
_____
_____
_____
_____
_____
_____

What is a storm surge? What might you find on the beach at the line of storm surge?

_____
_____
_____
_____
_____
_____
_____

# HEALTH/PHYSICAL EDUCATION

Jane Austen wrote about sea bathing in several of her novels. Bathing in the sea was seen as a curative for many ills in the Georgian Era of history. Research Sea Bathing. What were the benefits of this practice considered to be? Do you think that it truly was a curative for ills of the time? Why or why not?

_____

_____

_____

_____

_____

_____

_____

_____

Find a safe place to go swimming in the ocean.

Take a long, barefooted walk in the sand.

Play Frisbee at the beach.

# COMPUTER/LIBRARY SKILLS

You will use the internet and/or your local library for a great deal of the research for this unit study.

List the various resources you used during the course of your study.

Source Title                                                                Type of Media

_____

_____

_____

_____

_____

_____

_____

_____

_____

_____

_____

_____

_____

_____

_____

_____

_____

_____

_____

_____

_____

_____

_____

_____

_____

_____

_____

_____

_____

_____

_____

_____

_____

## FINE ARTS

Winslow Homer painted seascapes of Maine. Research and learn about Winslow Homer. Which of his works is your favorite?

_____

_____

_____

_____

_____

Research other Maine artists who create artwork with the sea as the subject. Who is your favorite? Why?

_____

_____

_____

_____

_____

Create your own seascape. Use a variety of mediums. Post a picture in the space b elow.

The ocean has its own symphony of sounds. List some of the different sounds you hear at the beach.

_____

_____

_____

_____

_____

# MAINE STUDIES

How many miles make up the Maine Coastline? _____

How many islands are there along the coast? _____

Are they all inhabited? Why or why not? _____
_____


Maine's rocky coast is home to harbor seals. The most famous being Andre. Research or read a book about Andre and record what you learned. You may also choose to watch the 1994 movie, *Andre*.

_____
_____
_____
_____
_____
_____
_____
_____
_____
_____
_____
_____
_____
_____
_____

# FIELD TRIPS

Take a trip to Maine State Aquarium.  Visit the website to plan in advance.
http://www.maine.gov/dmr/education/aquarium/index.html

What was your favorite sea creature at the aquarium?  What did you learn about it that you didn't already know?

_____

_____

_____

_____

_____

Take a trip to a sandy beach in Maine.  Where did you go?  What did you find?

_____

_____

_____

_____

_____

Take a trip to a rocky beach in Maine.  Where did you go?  What did you find?

_____

_____

_____

_____

_____

Compare and contrast the sandy beach and the rocky beach. Did you find the same types of shells/sea creatures at each? Why do you think parts of the coast have sandy beaches, while other parts are rocky?

_____

_____

_____

_____

_____

_____

# What I Learned

In this section, ask the student to narrate what they learned that they didn't know when they began this study. What new discovery did they make during the study? What did they enjoy most? What do they know now that they didn't know before? These are all good questions to ask, if the student needs prompting.

_____
_____
_____
_____
_____
_____
_____
_____
_____
_____
_____
_____
_____
_____
_____
_____
_____
_____
_____
_____
_____
_____
_____
_____
_____

Date Completed: _____

# ADDITIONAL RESOURCES

*At Home in the Tide Pool* – Wright, Alexandra & Peck III, Marshall

*One Small Square – Seashore* – Silver, Donald M.

*Seashells in My Pocket* – Hansen, Judith

*Seashells, Crabs and Sea Stars:  Take-Along Guide* – Tibbitts, Christiane Kump

*Marine Biology* – Apologia

www.homeschoolersofmaine.org

# Solution

```
M S E A L + + + + + + + + M E + + + K + + B + S
+ O L E S S U M + + + + + A L + + + + L A + E H
+ + O + + + + R + + + + + L K + + + + R E A + S
+ + + N + + T N A R O M R O C N + + + C + U H + I
+ + + + J + + + L + + + + + I + + T + R S + W F
+ + + + + E + + + L + + + W + I + C + E + + R
S + + + + + L + + + + O + + + I M + H + + A + + A
+ S + + + + + L + + + + D + + R + I + + + G + + T
+ + O + + + + + Y + + + D E E N + + + + U + + S
+ + + M + + + + + + + + H N P + + + + + L + + +
L + + + H + + + + + + + H + A + + + + + L + + +
+ O + + + S + + + + O + + + S + + + + + + + + +
+ + B + + + I + + + + R + + + R + + + + + + + +
K + + S + + + R + + S + + + + A + + + + + + + E
+ E + + T + + + I E + + + + + Z + + + + + L L +
+ + L + + E B + S + + + + + + O + + + + I C + +
+ + + P + A R H R O C K W E E D R + + + M A + + +
+ + + + R + O + + + + + + + + C + + P N + + + +
+ + + C + E + + + + + + + + + L + E R + + + + +
+ + + + C + + + + + + + + + + A T A + + + + + +
+ + + R + + + + + + + + + + + M B + + + + + + +
+ + A + + + S E A L E T T U C E + + + + + + + +
+ B + + + + + + + + + L L E H S R E P P I L S
+ + + + + + + + + + + + + + + + + + + + + + + +
+ + + + + + + + + + + + + + + + + + + + + + + +
```

(Over, Down, Direction)
BARNACLE (18,21,NE)
CLAM (15,4,N)
CORMORANT (15,4,W)
CRAB (4,19,NE)
HERMITCRAB (14,10,NE)
HORSESHOECRAB (14,11,SW)
IRISHMOSS (9,15,NW)
KELP (1,14,SE)
LIMPET (23,15,SW)
LOBSTER (1,11,SE)
MOONJELLY (1,1,SE)
MUSSEL (8,2,W)
PERIWINKLE (16,10,N)
RAZORCLAM (17,13,S)
ROCKWEED (9,17,E)
SANDDOLLAR (17,12,NW)
SEAGULL (22,5,S)
SEAL (2,1,E)
SEALETTUCE (7,22,E)
SEAURCHIN (25,1,SW)
SLIPPERSHELL (25,23,W)
STARFISH (25,9,N)
WHELK (24,5,NW)

# Maine Seabirds:

## Past & Present

Image by de zigeuner from Pixabay

# Table of Contents

## Before You Begin

Sometimes it can be challenging to figure out how to show progress when a student is working on a unit study. Before you begin this study, ask the student to give you a brief narrative of what they already know about the subject of this HOME unit study. Write this out for younger students, have older students write it out for themselves, here. When you finish the study, there is a page at the end entitled, **What I Learned,** for students to write down new things that they learned during the study. The comparison of these two pages can be used for portfolio reviews to document that progress in learning was made by the student.

_____
_____
_____
_____
_____
_____
_____
_____
_____
_____
_____
_____
_____
_____
_____
_____
_____
_____
_____
_____
_____
_____
_____
_____
_____
_____

Date Begun: _____

## BIBLE

Explore the book of Genesis to discover what day penguins, and other birds and sea creatures, were created on.

_____
_____
_____
_____

How many different birds are listed in the Bible?  Are any of them similar to birds that inhabit the coast of Maine?

_____
_____
_____
_____
_____

Choose a passage of Scripture that is related to a bird.  Write it out for copy work/penmanship.  Memorize it. Share it with others.

_____
_____
_____
_____
_____

# MATH

For students who enjoy online learning games, there is a fun multiplication game (Penguin Jump) available at this website: http://www.mathplayground.com/ASB_PenguinJumpMultiplication.html.

Compare the different wing spans of the various Maine seabirds. Using a cloth tape measure, compare the wing span to things in your house and yard, for instance, your couch, bed, or car.

| Bird | Wingspan | Comparable household item |
|------|----------|---------------------------|
|      |          |                           |
|      |          |                           |
|      |          |                           |
|      |          |                           |
|      |          |                           |

Spend some time at one or more beaches, and take a survey of the various seabirds that are present. Repeat this on several occasions to compare the numbers present on different days. Create graphs reflecting your findings.

|  |  |  |  |  |  |  |
|--|--|--|--|--|--|--|
|  |  |  |  |  |  |  |

## LANGUAGE ARTS

Read the story *Mr. Poppers Penguins*. This can be read independently by the student or as a family read aloud. After reading the story, watch the movie by the same title. Have students compare and contrast the two stories.

_____
_____
_____
_____
_____
_____
_____
_____
_____

Choose from among the list of children's books about seabirds. Read and write a brief book report.

*Birds Vs. Blades: Offshore Wind Power and the Race to Protect Seabirds* by Rebecca E. Hirsch

*(The) Burgess Seashore Book for Children* by Thornton Burgess

*(The) Eagle and the Seagulls: A Wisdom Story for Children & Adults* by James L. Capra

*(The) Ladybird Book of Sea & Estuary Birds* by John Leigh-Pemberton

*Looking for Seabirds: Journal of an Alaskan Voyage* by Sophie Webb

*Puffin Peter* by Petr Horacek

*Pufflings* by Margaret Wild

*Salty Seagull: A Tale of an Old Salt* by Suzanne Tate

*Samantha Seagull's Sandals* by Gordon Winch

*Seabird* by Holling C. Holling

*Seacrow Island* by Astrid Lindgren

*Sea Gull* by Danny Snell

*Seagull by the Shore: The Story of a Herring Gull* by Vanessa Giancamilli

*Skye the Puffling* by Lynne Rickards

*Sparrow, Eagle, Penguin and Seagull: What is a Bird?* by Brian P. Cleary

# Book Report Page

Title: _____

Author: _____

Illustrator: _____

Publisher: _____


Main character(s) in the story: _____

_____


Where does the story take place: _____

_____


What happens during the story: _____

_____

_____

_____


Would you recommend this story to a friend?  Why or why not? _____

_____

_____

_____

NOTES:

# Maine Seabirds Word Find

```
F I L I B T R M E S O O G D I
U X B G C Z Z D O M Z X U F Z
Q X U O W F A W I C W Q I C N
D B R O Y B V C S U E L L O J
V C X P N B H U N A L Q L K J
A U W M A Q U M J I R L E F N
W G C W J L O D B P U Z M K I
T F Y P G S U R P G C G O H F
H H B N B C O R M O R A N T F
E F Z H K Z Y U R B C Z T E U
L A T Z A W L P E J R E P I P
C J A R S U W D T M R W G D Z
D Y G T A Z K C N N X Y V E X
K U F C D A T A P Z C N T R X
K R O Y C P Z J A K Z I P L Y
```

Locate the following words in the word search above.  Words may go forward, backward or diagonally.   If any of them are unfamiliar, look up the meaning in a dictionary or online.

AUK
CORMORANT
CURLEW
DUCK
EIDER
GOOSE
GUILLEMONT
GULL
PENGUIN
PIPER
PUFFIN
RAZORBILL
TERN

NOTES:

# SOCIAL STUDIES

Read *My Season With Penguins: An Antarctic Journal*. Have students imagine spending time with penguins and write their own journal about their experience.

_____
_____
_____
_____
_____
_____
_____

Read *Testimony of Some Early Voyagers on the Great Auk* by Fanny Hardy.   A copy can be downloaded here: https://www.jstor.org/tc/accept?origin=/stable/pdf/4066985.pdf

_____
_____
_____
_____
_____

Research Project Puffin and record what you learned.

When was it established, and by whom? What is the purpose of Project Puffin? Are puffins the only Maine sea bird that biologists are attempting to restore?

_____
_____
_____
_____
_____
_____
_____
_____
_____

# SCIENCE

The Great Auk was a penguin like seabird that once inhabited Maine's shores. It is now extinct. Discuss why you think the Great Auk became extinct. Research it to see if you are correct.

_____
_____
_____
_____
_____
_____

There has been discussion of using DNA from fossils and preserved remains to reintroduce the Great Auk. Do you think this is a good idea? What are the environmental implications of such a project?

http://www.telegraph.co.uk/science/2016/08/19/plot-hatched-to-reintroduce-extinct-great-auk-to-british-shores/
_____
_____
_____
_____
_____

Choose one seabird to research and write a brief report about.

_____
_____
_____
_____
_____
_____
_____
_____
_____
_____
_____
_____
_____
_____

Visit the website Easy Science for Kids, and complete their free, interactive seabird quiz.
http://easyscienceforkids.com/free-interactive-sea-birds-quiz-fun-quizzes-for-kids-online/

Define the following words:

Extinct: _____

_____

Endangered: _____

_____

Threatened: _____

_____

Special Concerns: _____

_____


Consider each one of these in relation to seabirds in Maine.  Do we currently have any seabirds that are extinct, endangered, threatened, or that there are special concerns about?  Why or why not?  If there are, what can the average citizen do to protect these Maine treasures?

_____

_____

_____

_____

_____

_____


Discuss the benefits of wind power and consider the impact on seabirds.  Does the benefit outweigh the detriment?  What can be done so that we can benefit from wind power, while reducing the impact on seabirds?

_____

_____

_____

_____

_____

## HEALTH/PHYSICAL EDUCATION

Observe seabirds at the shore, or watch video clips of their movements.  Create your own seabird dance by combining the various movements, walking, soaring, preening, etc..

Learn about what different seabirds eat.   Would you consider eating the same food as a seabird for a meal?  Do you already share in some of the same foods that they eat?

_____

_____

_____

_____

_____

_____

Visit the ocean during the winter.  Feel the water temperature.  Discuss hypothermia and what would happen to humans if they swam in water the same temperature that penguins swim in.

_____

_____

_____

_____

_____

_____

# COMPUTER/LIBRARY SKILLS

You will use the internet and/or your local library for a great deal of the research for this unit study.

List the various resources you used during the course of your study.

Source Title                                                                 Type of Media

_____

_____

_____

_____

_____

_____

_____

_____

_____

_____

_____

_____

_____

_____

_____

_____

_____

_____

_____

_____

_____

_____

_____

_____

_____

_____

_____

_____

_____

_____

_____

## FINE ARTS

Paint with feathers.  How is it different than painting with a brush or sponges?  How is it similar?

_____
_____
_____
_____
_____

Study the work and art of John James Audubon. Write a brief report of his life and work.

_____
_____
_____
_____
_____
_____
_____
_____
_____
_____
_____
_____
_____
_____
_____
_____
_____
_____
_____
_____

# FOREIGN LANGUAGE

Look up and learn the different Latin names for the different types of seabirds in Maine. What is your favorite and why?

| Seabird | Latin Name |
|---------|------------|
|         |            |
|         |            |
|         |            |
|         |            |
|         |            |
|         |            |
|         |            |

# MAINE STUDIES

What is a shorebird? _____

Is a gull a shorebird? _____


Why is Maine important for shorebirds? _____

_____

_____

_____


Choose one of Maine's shorebirds and write about its migratory pattern, when it inhabits Maine, what type of habitat it needs for nesting, etc.

_____

_____

_____

_____

_____

_____

_____

_____

_____

_____

_____

_____

_____

_____

_____

_____

_____

_____

_____

## FIELD TRIPS

Project Puffin Visitor Center, Rockland, Maine
http://projectpuffin.audubon.org/visit-us/puffin-tours

Any local park or beach on the shore of the Maine coast.

Consider going on a puffin cruise.
https://www.boothbayboattrips.com/cruises/puffin-scenic-cruise/

Record your experiences below:

_____
_____
_____
_____
_____
_____
_____
_____
_____
_____
_____
_____
_____
_____
_____
_____
_____
_____

NOTES:

## What I Learned

In this section, ask the student to narrate what they learned that they didn't know when they began this study. What new discovery did they make during the study? What did they enjoy most? What do they know now that they didn't know before? These are all good questions to ask, if the student needs prompting.

_____
_____
_____
_____
_____
_____
_____
_____
_____
_____
_____
_____
_____
_____
_____
_____
_____
_____
_____
_____
_____
_____
_____
_____
_____
_____
_____
_____

Date Completed: _____

NOTES:

**Website Resources**

https://www.maine.gov/ifw/fish-wildlife/wildlife/species-information/birds/shorebirds.html

https://answersingenesis.org/birds/penguins/

https://www.penguinwatch.org/#/

https://kids.kiddle.co/Penguin

http://www.livescience.com/27434-penguin-facts.html

http://extinct-animals-facts.com/Recently-Extinct-Animal-Facts/Extinct-Great-Auk-Facts.html

http://johnjames.audubon.org/extinction-great-auk

# Sea Glass

## Table of Contents

## Before You Begin

Sometimes it can be challenging to figure out how to show progress when a student is working on a unit study. Before you begin this study, ask the student to give you a brief narrative of what they already know about the subject of this HOME unit study. Write this out for younger students, have older students write it out for themselves, here. When you finish the study, there is a page at the end entitled, **What I Learned,** for students to write down new things that they learned during the study. The comparison of these two pages can be used for portfolio reviews to document that progress in learning was made by the student.

_____
_____
_____
_____
_____
_____
_____
_____
_____
_____
_____
_____
_____
_____
_____
_____
_____
_____
_____
_____
_____
_____
_____
_____
_____

Date Begun: _____

# BIBLE

Define the word refined: _____

_____

It takes time and being rolled in the salty, ocean water against the sand and the rocks to turn broken glass into beautifully frosted sea glass.  It takes God time and refining to turn us from a broken shard into something beautiful.

What are some Bible passages that talk about God refining his people?

_____
_____
_____
_____
_____
_____

Use the ideas from the link below to create Biblical applications for your children from sea glass.

http://www.parentinglikehannah.com/2018/02/what-sea-glass-can-teach-your-kids-about-god.html

# MATH

Using stones, sea glass and shells from the beach, create a three dimensional picture or mosaic. Mosaic Art affords some concrete learning opportunities for children. It can assist in the development of:

Counting

Sorting

Matching

Assembling

Problem Solving

Logic

Perception

Spatial & Visual Organization

Calculation of Surface Area

and so much more!!

Post pictures of your creations below.

# LANGUAGE ARTS

Discuss what a legend is.  Look up *The Legend of Sea Glass*, sometimes called, *The Mermaids Tear*.  Write your own legend about sea glass.

_____

_____

_____

_____

_____

_____

_____

Read a book about sea glass and write a book report.

**Suggested Reading List**

*Journey of the Sea Glass* by Nicole Fazio

*Max, Mollie and the Magic of Sea Glass:  A Lesson in Character* by Ardis Glace

*S is for Sea Glass:  A Beach Alphabet* by Richard Michelson

*Sea Glass:  Golden Mountain Chronicles: 1970* by Laurence Yep

*Seaglass Summer* by Anjali Banerjee

*Seaglass Tales* by Summer Stone

*The Story of the Sea Glass* by Anne Wescott Dodd

# Book Report Page

Title: _____

Author: _____

Illustrator: _____

Publisher: _____


Main character(s) in the story: _____

_____


Where does the story take place: _____

_____


What happens during the story: _____

_____

_____

_____


Would you recommend this story to a friend?  Why or why not? _____

_____

_____

_____

# SOCIAL STUDIES

Using the list of beaches where sea glass can be found in the Field Trip section of this unit study, create a map of Maine marking all these points.

Why is true or natural sea glass so hard to find? Do you think people should be allowed to pick sea glass from the beach and take it home? Why or why not? Write a brief essay, both for and against people being able to pick and keep sea glass.

_____

_____

_____

_____

_____

_____

_____

_____

_____

_____

_____

_____


Should people be allowed to smash colored glass on the beach to help create a constant supply of sea glass? Why or why not? Give an oral presentation presenting your point of view. Create an outline for your presentation below.

# SCIENCE

Research the process required in nature to create natural sea glass. Compare it to the process by which man made sea glass can be created.

_____
_____
_____
_____
_____
_____

Why is that old, clear glass turns purple/amethyst in color?

_____
_____
_____
_____
_____

How is glass made?

_____
_____
_____
_____
_____
_____
_____

# HEALTH/PHYSICAL EDUCATION

Take a walk along a beach searching for sea glass.  Track how far you walk during your search.

_____

_____

_____

_____

_____


In the 19th century, doctors often advised people who were unwell to spend time by the sea.  Do you think that being near the sea actually has healing properties?  Why or why not?

_____

_____

_____

_____

_____

_____

_____

_____

_____

# COMPUTER/LIBRARY SKILLS

You will use the internet and/or your local library for a great deal of the research for this unit study.

List the various resources you used during the course of your study.

Source Title                                                                    Type of Media

_____

_____

_____

_____

_____

_____

_____

_____

_____

_____

_____

_____

_____

_____

_____

_____

_____

_____

_____

_____

_____

_____

_____

_____

_____

_____

_____

_____

_____

_____

_____

# FINE ARTS

Visit a jewelry store of gift shop that has sea glass jewelry. Learn something about the craftsman who created the pieces that are on display.

_____
_____
_____
_____
_____
_____

If you find sea glass on a beach visit, learn how to wrap it to create your own jewelry.

_____
_____
_____
_____
_____
_____
_____

Choose different shapes/colors of sea glass to create a picture.

NOTES:

# MAINE STUDIES

Read *Sea glass hunting uncovers bits of Maine's* past at the link below.

https://bangordailynews.com/2017/11/24/living/sea-glass-hunting-uncovers-bits-of-maines-past/

What did you learn? _____

_____

_____

_____

_____

_____

_____

_____

_____

_____

_____

_____

_____

Search for pieces of pottery on your next beach walk. If you find one, describe it and write a fictional account of where it came from and how it might have gotten there.

_____

_____

_____

_____

_____

_____

_____

_____

_____

_____

_____

_____

_____

_____

_____

# FIELD TRIPS

Below is a list of beaches around Maine that are known for their beach glass. The best time to visit is in the early spring, after the winter storms, but before tourists have begun their seasonal visits. March to May is the best time for this.

## Acadia/Downeast Area

Sand Beach, Acadia National Park

Frenchman's Bay, Acadia National Park

Rogue Bluffs State Park

Mowery Beach

South Lubec Beach

Jasper Beach

McLellan Park

Cranberry Island

## MidCoast Maine

Heads Beach, Phippsburg

Fort Popham

Belfast Beach

Boothbay Harbor

Brunswick's Lands End

Lincolnville Beach

Fish Beach, Monhegan Island

Mackerel Cove, Bailey's Island

## Portland/Casco Bay

Peaks Island

## Southern Coast

Middle Beach, Kennebunkport

Spring Point Beach, South Portland

Find an artisan near you who does glass blowing and arrange for a visit.

# Field Trip Form

**Date:** _____

**Destination:** _____

**Purpose:** _____

**Something I saw or learned:**

_____
_____
_____
_____
_____
_____
_____
_____

Insert or draw a picture here from your field trip:

NOTES:

## What I Learned

In this section, ask the student to narrate what they learned that they didn't know when they began this study. What new discovery did they make during the study? What did they enjoy most? What do they know now that they didn't know before? These are all good questions to ask, if the student needs prompting.

_____
_____
_____
_____
_____
_____
_____
_____
_____
_____
_____
_____
_____
_____
_____
_____
_____
_____
_____
_____
_____
_____
_____
_____
_____
_____
_____

Date Completed: _____

Made in United States
North Haven, CT
24 March 2022

17496827R00063